Still Breathing

HOW TO REGAIN YOUR LIFE AFTER BEING ROBBED

Joe Braxton

Copyright © 2017 Joe Braxton
All rights reserved.

ISBN: 1530813638
ISBN 13: 9781530813636
Library of Congress Control Number: 2016914905
CreateSpace Independent Publishing Platform
North Charleston, South Carolina

Dedication

I dedicate my book to my beautiful mom, Cynthia Keaton; to my beautiful godmother, Margaret "Poochie" Jennings, who's no longer with us; and to anyone else who's on a path to find the light at the end of his or her journey. Mom, I just want to say that your strength is what gets me through. I know it's been a rocky road for you, for me, and for us as a whole. I sit back sometimes and think about some of my past transgressions, and I somehow can't forgive myself for all that I've put you through. I want you to know that I was more running from myself. Today, I can actually stand on my own two feet as a stronger man than I was before. I'm on the right path in life now, and I want to continue to make you proud of me. I appreciate the fact that you never left my side. I want you to live the life that you've always wanted to, and know that I have always believed in you and always will. Thanks for being my rock, and I love you to the moon and back.

I am truly blessed to have had the opportunity to experience multiple examples of motherly love. Poochie, when you left us I was twelve years old, and a piece of me left with you. I know that throughout the years you've been the angel on our shoulders. Not just mine, but Cornelius's and Yolanda's as well. At a young age, you opened my eyes and heart to blind awareness, and I often tried to put myself in your shoes; however, it was only to imagine what you actually went through. That's why now I have no problem with empathizing as well as showing compassion for others. I miss you and love you so much.

Last but not least, I would like to say thank you, Wanda.

To my readers, I appreciate you and would like you to appreciate yourself and others.

> *"For his anger endureth but a moment; in his favour is life: weeping may endure for a night, but joy cometh in the morning."*

(Ps. 30:5)

Giving Thanks

I would like to take this time to give thanks to all my friends who helped make my dream of becoming an author possible with all their cooperation; your assistance will never go unnoticed.

Cover photo: Jackie Hicks (Fond Memories)
Back-cover photo: Weikerken Altema (Surpass Visuals)
Barber: Adam (Petie) Wilder (Ebony Barbers)

Still Breathing

In a world full of skepticism and prudence, it's hard to find your identity. We all know who we were born as; however, who we end up being is a different story. For instance, I was born Joseph Braxton, consistent supporter, compassionate friend, and family member. Some people would even describe me as an extremely engaging fella. I'm the guy everyone wants to be around—even though they can't seem to figure me out. Well, here's the thing; I'm still trying to figure out who I am and what my purpose is in life. Part of who I am has been masked by pain for twenty-four long years.

My story is one that I never thought I would find the courage to tell. With that being said, my name, once again, is Joseph Braxton, and I am a survivor of molestation. And while I have your attention, and the courage to finish my story, I ask you to brace yourself, because what I'm about to share with you is the truth, the whole truth, and nothing but the truth, so help me God…

I was small; I was helpless, and I was afraid. I was alone; I was small; I was helpless, and *I was afraid*…

I was resting peacefully in my nice, clean, animated pajamas with matching underwear. Perhaps I was even dreaming, but that I'm not sure of. Regardless, I wasn't prepared to be robbed of my youth, by an uncle of a friend. My friend's name was Tory, and we would play like there was no tomorrow. I knew his family, and they treated me like I was a part of it. His uncle's name was Robby. He stood about six feet tall, or maybe it just seemed that way because I was such a small child.

One night, when I was eleven, Uncle Robby, which is what I was told I could call him, came into the room and got in the bed alongside me. As I said before, I was resting peacefully, not a care in the world. The next thing I knew, my underwear was being pulled aggressively around my knees. I felt a sudden sense of panic approaching my lungs. I had been abruptly woken out of my slumber and was feeling confused as to why it was happening. Unable to adjust my body to see what was going on, I realized he had my hands pinned behind my back. Uncle Robby stretched toward the dresser and reached for some baby oil. Without any warning I felt a sudden thrust of agonizing pain inside me. He covered my mouth so that no one would hear me scream. The pain was endless, indescribable, to say the least. A family member came to the door and asked about the constant noise. I lied and said we were wrestling, out of fear.

By the grace of God, I found the strength to break free from his grasp. After that, I ran as fast as I could toward the bedroom door, only to find that my vicious victimizer had locked it. I began to cry profusely from the overwhelming pain and confusion. I was only eleven; why would I think that I needed to protect myself from an adult, who on occasion had protected me? I used to envy Tory for having so many male role models in his life whom he could look up to, men who could offer him guidance when necessary. My thought pattern changed once his uncle robbed me of my innocence. It became very difficult to be around Tory and act as if nothing had happened. It wasn't like I could tell him what I had been through. All I could think about for days was the fact that Robby had said to me that if I ever told anyone, I would end up on the back of a milk carton.

I've asked God so many times why this happened to me. I was a child being threatened by an adult. Why did he feel the need to not only rob me of my childhood but also place fear in my heart? What had I ever done to him to make him hate me so much? Enough hate to want to partake in ruining my life. I felt like I was being punished for wrongdoing. Awkwardly enough, that wasn't the case; I was the innocent one. This man had created a pain in my soul that I thought I would never recover from. How would I begin to heal from something so tragic? Where was my superhero, the one whom I used to read about in all the comic books and watch in all the animated movies? Who was going to come and rescue me from all that I had been through? *No one!*

I became frustrated and angry at the fact that I couldn't go and ask for help. I was left in solitude; I was mentally alone. What made him do this to me? That was the question I asked myself all the time. I wanted to escape from myself and from him. He didn't just let me be after the first time; this became an ongoing vicious cycle. Every time he touched me, I felt like I was taking my last breath. I'd seen this man with several women, and yet he still found the need to abuse me. I constantly found myself trying to figure out how was I still going to be Tory's friend while dealing with my current situation. Every time I thought about it, the answer was the same: I wasn't afraid of Tory, but I was terrified of his uncle. It hurt me to my heart to have to stop being friends with a boy who was like a brother to me. I had no choice in the matter; every time Robby found out that I was staying over Tory's house, he would come over and rape me again.

Growing up, I heard many stories about how mentally unstable Robby was. When you're young you trust easily; therefore, you believe anything. I was considered to be an introverted young man who showed signs of being a bit timid. Predators find people of that nature easy targets for malicious acts of violence. Robby knew once he threatened me that I would be too afraid to go against anything he told me to do. At a young age, I was taught that a person can look at you and tell how far they can go with you. One thing's for sure: he definitely preyed on my innocence. He took it and wrapped it around his little finger. I did whatever he told me to do; I was too afraid not to. He trained me to become what he wanted me to be, a female companion. I was a little boy being taught how to perform fellatio on my friend's uncle. I didn't understand why, when he had his pick of actual female companions. Ones who probably would have done all the things he was asking me to do. How disturbing was that for a child my age?

After I performed oral sex on him the first time, he started calling me his girlfriend. He turned me into the person he now craved sexual attention from. This man was trying to control my feelings and my thinking patterns. He would be in a relationship with others and try to deal with me at the same time. He would bring his girlfriends over to Tory's house, and while they were visiting with Tory's family, he would try to make out with me in another room. Every time we did any sexual act, I made myself feel like nothing, just to make him feel like he was everything.

Guys like Robby who carry themselves in that manner are considered to be DL (down low) brothers—men who are living full-fledged heterosexual lifestyles but are discreetly interested in same-sex encounters. Those are the type of guys whom I now seem to be attracted to. Damn him for instilling something in me that otherwise I may not have been into. But because of him, I grew this fascination for straight men. I would only want the ones who already had girlfriends or wives. I never felt like I was worthy of having a relationship that I could call my own. And although I didn't agree with what Robby was doing to his family, I would never say anything to anyone about it. Fear will stop you from doing many things in life. I often wondered how Robby was able to go home every night after one of our sexual sessions, kiss his children on the forehead, and then get into bed with his wife. I wasn't bothered by it at first, because I felt like he really wanted to be with me. When I was with him, I felt safe; away from him, I didn't know what he was planning to do to me. I would never tell him where I lived; then last year I gave him my address. I was extremely bothered by the fact that I did, but I couldn't seem to escape from the fear of him. Every time this man called, I felt like I was obligated to take care of his needs. In some ways, I felt like I was in need of something.

My father wasn't really in my life, and I yearned for stability and a man's strength. I had nowhere else to get it from. I eventually started filling the void with Robby's malicious acts of aggressiveness. Instead of being upset by his presence, I started feeling a sense of fulfillment. I eventually fell in love with what I knew he was offering me, even if it wasn't right. It was his strength, his masculinity, and his dominance that won me over. After a while, I believed that maybe I was wrong—did he love me, and that's why he caused me so much pain? You have to understand; this is where he left me mentally night after night. I was mentally and physically trapped by this horrible situation. It had completely suffocated my way of living. This ordeal left me continuously confused. I started feeling like I was being brainwashed. I was now a permanent fixture in this man's life.

As time went on, my feelings for him grew stronger and stronger. I knew I was a boy, but when he called me his girl, in some ways it kind of made me feel like I was. My reasoning for this came from how he treated me when we were alone. I was his sex toy on and off for approximately twenty-four years. I never stopped being afraid of him. And, he never stopped reminding me that he would kill me if I ever told a soul. I felt like a person living in a straitjacket. All I knew was that I was his—and his only. I tried talking to him on numerous occasions about why he chose me. His response was always, "You never stopped me." I was baffled by his answer. I never wanted anything like this to happen; it was forced upon me! It was as if he robbed me of my choice to decide whether or not I wanted to be this way. Still, to this day, it's hard for me to determine whether I'm gay or straight. When identifying as gay, they say you don't have the choice to change your decision. God gave us all free will to be who we are. Sometimes I hate men! Having sex at times becomes awkward for me. I have to be emotionally attached in order to feel good about an intimate encounter. Also, because of years of being forced by Robby to perform certain sexual acts, every time I have sex now, I need to be in a hostile setting.

My relationships over the years have been very abusive. I couldn't figure out why my level of self-worth was so low. After a while I started feeling like if I wasn't being mistreated, then the person didn't love me. I often looked for men who had Robby's characteristic traits. I never stopped wondering why I was the chosen one. Did someone do this to him? Was he sexually molested as a child or an adolescent? I built a wall that I've kept up almost all my life. I've been asked on several occasions, "Why are you so quiet; are you a mute?" My reply would always be, "No, I'm just a little shy." I realize now that it was because I was constantly made to feel inadequate, which in turn made me afraid to speak my mind. I was robbed of many precious things during my life: my innocence, my childhood, and my voice most of all. I felt unworthy, ashamed, confused, used, and embarrassed, so I chose to keep it all buried inside.

I want my readers to know that this story wasn't written to incriminate anyone. It's my story, and I needed to tell it. I've been depressed and living behind a wall of shame and hurt for too long. I can't live like this anymore. I've lost a part of me that I'll never be able to regain, but from here on, I've chosen to take charge of my life. I have cried a river of tears, and underneath the waves I found the strength to let the water wash me clean. I am beyond ready to sail into my new life. I know that to some these words I speak may not matter, but for me this story has helped me heal from something that almost killed me. I want to be able to enjoy beautiful sunsets, whether it's with a man or a woman. I just want to feel normal again.

I've always felt like Robby held me captive all these years. I've been cruising through life making the most careless decisions and following the wrong crowds, all in search of a mental diversion to fill the void I was carrying in my heart. I was broken by the molestation. I no longer wanted to feel the pain or let the thoughts of it cause me mental agony. I did things that I knew weren't right, like breaking the law. I'm not a criminal who belongs behind bars or in any institution. I'm just a man who was stripped of everything he held sacred. I watched people talk to each other all my life. I sat in a crowded room silent and very much alone. I don't want to be alone anymore; I want what others have. All the life experiences I've had have been based off being victimized. I never truly knew how to act around others. It didn't feel adequate to have a good time. The way people acted around me didn't feel real. They were actually nice and caring, something I wasn't used to. To talk is a gift, and to tell someone how you feel is a miracle. Don't ever let anyone take that from you.

During that very silent period of time, I also kept being faced with thoughts of my sexuality. Was I really gay, or did I just like having a man around for strength and security? I've been stuck in a twenty-four-year abusive relationship. I learned early on that Robby was the type of guy who would kill his mate if that person ever tried to leave him. For that reason alone, I could never fully give myself to anyone else. I've always felt like I was his and his only. This man had taken what belonged to me.

I often wonder what my life would be like today if this hadn't happened to me. Last year it hit me: it's time to let go of my past and be free! I wanted to be able to smile authentically again. It was time to start living a happier life and let down the wall that had stunted my growth for so long. I decided to be free from Robby's bondage. This man had chosen my sexuality for me. I was determined that he wasn't going to take anything else.

As time went on, I became a socialite in the DMV area. I knew I had to do something to break the chains that he had around me. I didn't care much for being at home alone. I constantly found myself in a state of depression. Being around other people made me forget about the pain I was in. I used alcohol as a pain reliever as well. No one around me knew that I was holding trauma deep inside me. Even though I decided to regain my strength and let go of all this madness, I still longed for the fatherly love that I had never received. I decided to become a father figure to others in need. I started volunteering and supporting other groups. And even though some people didn't care much for me, my feelings for them were genuine. What I was doing helped me temporarily ease the pain. Through it all I still loved Robby, but I hated him for what he had done to me. This is the mental capacity of a victim of molestation. The confusion never leaves your heart or your mind.

As I've grown into the man I am today, I finally realize that I'm not alone in this. Sometimes in life we can be our own worst critic. There are so many people in the world who have experienced what I have, just in a different capacity. My advice to anyone who will listen is to get help as soon as it happens. Remember, there is always something or someone that can slow a predator down. A predator's strength is only as strong as his victim's fear.

Through it all, I discovered that I was unredeemed. I didn't know I was, until so many things in my life began to suffer as a result of it. My finances began dwindling; I wasn't hanging out with my friends as often as I used to; I stopped inviting people over, and I decided to compartmentalize my apartment. I no longer wanted to sleep in my bedroom, so I slept in the den on my sofa. I was determined that in some way, form, or fashion, I would get rid of the lingering memories. And thank God for county and state resources, or I would have been homeless. To show my gratitude to the Lord for saving me from such a mind-boggling situation, I try to volunteer almost every Sunday to feed the homeless.

The key to surviving molestation is learning to live beyond your pain. No one can ever tell you when to get over what you've been through. Only you can determine when the healing process begins. Most of all, you have to remove the people from your life who are there only to pass judgment. Never allow a person on the outside looking in to analyze your triumph or your struggle. Everyone must find a way to cope with whatever it is they're going through, whether it's rape, molestation, a deadly disease, or an abusive relationship.

All this time, no one knew that I had been raped or molested. These events were extremely detrimental to my life and my inner peace. I tried to pretend that my tragedy didn't affect me, mainly because I didn't want it to. I even convinced myself that I could handle it on my own.

I wasn't really into discussing my business with others, especially something so painful. I was too busy trying to search for a way to forget it myself; why would I want to discuss it? I learned early on that I never would be able to dismiss it from my mind. Forgiveness was the concept that I overlooked. It wasn't until my relationship with God got stronger that I realized that I needed to forgive my victimizer in order to properly move on. I often wonder if that opened a door for tragedy to continue to strike my life—a door that will never be opened again as long as God is my protector.

Molestation is something that can weigh on you mentally. Just as importantly, you can lose who you are in the process. There were many things that suffered in my life as a result of it: my finances, my relationships, and my eating habits. I stopped going to the gym, and consequently I gained forty pounds. It can literally harden your emotions if you let it. I always felt like I needed to have my guard up. After what happened to me, trust was no longer in my vocabulary. I drifted into a black hole, and depression became my disability. In December 2015, a close friend talked to me about my life and how it made them feel. I knew I had to snap out of it. Of course, it was easier said than done, but I knew I had to do something. I came up with an idea to get into arts and crafts. I started making decorative pendants for the lapels of suit jackets. Music also became a therapeutic antidote for me. I thank all these artists Mariah Carey, Michael and Janet Jackson, Phyllis Hyman,

Erica Campbell, Vashawn Mitchell, Lalah Hathaway, Patti Labelle, Yolanda Adams, and Toni Braxton. They all were influential in lifting me up.

You know what I figured out? That deep down inside of us all is a lioness or lion that is dying to let out the most powerful roar. Personally, I believe that the best time to release it is when everything in you knows that you're being violated against your will. I extend this word of wisdom to you all, because the more I relive what I've been through, the more I wish I had found my inner lion sooner.

If you're not careful, criticism, pain, and disappointment will become a permanent fixture in your life. Praise and acknowledgment will feel uncomfortable, because you won't think that you deserve it. There is not one person in this world who has earned that much power over your life. Anyone who shames you for your truth is ultimately trying to shift the attention away from their own. God did not intend for us all to be exactly the same. His sole purpose in creating us was so that we could exist in this world as unique individuals. Everything that has happened to you is divinely perfected for where God is taking you. I for one have been where you are. There will definitely be times when you'll get discouraged, even afraid. The remedy for those human emotions will always be prayer. Although my battle with sexual abuse is far from over, I'm willing to get up every day and try. I know some people will read my story and say to themselves, "That will never happen to me." My advice to you is, "Never say never."

Even though my tragedy happened many years ago, in my heart of hearts it feels like yesterday. When you go through something as traumatic as sexual abuse, triggers become attached to your healing process. What I mean by that is that there will be times when you will be faced with certain reminders of what you've been through. These can include movies or television shows that feature a series on sexual predators, or public testimonies of sexual assault. Here's where your true strength comes in; this is the part of the recovery process that will force you to decide whether or not you will allow yourself to be released from those hostile chains. It already takes long enough to gain the courage to live outside the predator's grasp. Please don't allow a setback of any kind to disturb your self-improvement.

If nothing else, I've learned that there is noise in silence. Some people are afraid to communicate, and because of that they fail in relationships of all kinds. I promised myself that my quiet time would be over if I ever gained the courage to speak up even once. I prayed to God on many nights for a voice of my own. Having a voice is not the same as talking. A voice gives you the gumption to make people hear you; no matter who you are or what you've been through, they will listen. It will be in their spirit and in their heart to give you a chance to redeem yourself. The ability to speak on subjects such as this one comes from your experiences and compassion. Don't wait until something drastic happens to learn compassion; start now. I've always felt that the most inconsiderate people are those who are judgmental. I could be wrong; that's just my opinion. There's a saying that goes, "Don't judge me for my choices when you don't understand my reasons." That is a motto that I live by, because many are out here doing the same things they fault you for. If more people in the world could face their own truths and stop basing their lives on yours, the world would be a better place. The goal in life is not to pretend that you're perfect but to perfect the best version of yourself.

Some people will love you only if you fit into their box; don't be afraid to disappoint. Many times when you change who you are to please others, it's for people unconcerned with your well-being. Their effort is solely based on throwing you off your game while they succeed at their own. Stay true to your focus, which is learning to live through sexual abuse. In order to help others live past their assaults, I had to find a way to live past my own. This tragedy had me breaking while resting. Every day I'm learning still, but I'm clearly on my way. There have been days where I've had to pick myself up piece by piece. Some days are better than others, but I won't ever stop fighting for all of me. I know that I won't ever get my childhood back; I lost out on the years that were supposed to be an important part of growing up. That part of life was given to me by God to help mold me into the man I was originally created to be. Don't get me wrong; I don't regret any of the lessons I've learned.

However, I'm willing to bet that the sexual assault wasn't part of his original plan for my life.

God has kept me wrapped in his grace. I was introduced to his power through my pain. Now that I know him like I do, I don't even know how I ever lived without him. My everyday get-up-and-go was instilled in me by him. God has made his appearance known in my dreams, to disappoint the devil during my nightmares. I must devote all my time and attention to him. I am forever pleased to do the work of God. I was lost; I was beyond misplaced in life. I have always felt like I've been just going with the flow. My life has never felt like my own. All the pain that I've endured will slowly but surely be put to rest. That is a prayer that God has promised to answer. All I have to do is continue to walk in faith. My faith in God is real to me, and nothing real can be threatened. Let the essence of beauty pierce your spirit, your heart, and your mind. God is beautiful; represent him well. Somebody somewhere is depending on you to do what God has called you to do. Trust that your faith will guide you through it.

From sunup to sundown, I'm constantly thinking of ways that I can help better my community. There's a saying: "It takes a village to raise a family." I also believe it takes a village to better a community; I just want to be a part of the result. "Not everything that can be counted counts…and not everything that counts can be counted." I plan on being a part of the equation that counts the most. Helping others has been poured into my veins through a spiritual transfusion; I'm not looking for a sinful flush. The things I do are not just to help others but to help better myself as well. All the time and attention that I offer has always been something that I've wanted for myself. I'm praying that by participating in God's plan for me, I will eventually gain the respect from others that I deserve. In the past I've been mistreated, taken advantage of, and lied to. I could have easily become bitter and hostile; however, I've always chosen to be the better person. When others mistreat you, walk away, smile, and keep being you; it's worked for me all this time. I forgive but never forget, because I never want to be hurt the same way twice.

Within my experience of sexual abuse, I found myself drifting into a state of seclusion. I believe at some point in my life I underestimated what I was capable of. I didn't know what to do with the new pieces of my life. I felt forever stuck in that abused state of mind. It's hard to constantly walk around unbothered. I'm a man who was raped repeatedly by a person I thought was trustworthy. I'm blessed to still be alive after all that has happened to me. My sexual abuse caused my life to spiral into a living hell. Sometimes every part of me aches from the painful distress. I use the laughter of others to drown out the memories of my victimizer. I often wonder if the people I socialize with are laughing at me or with me. I had to realize that living with those types of feelings inside me makes me a little difficult to be around. My trust in others has been tainted more than once. One thing I try to help others with is finding a way to understand, accept, and appreciate the fact that they are one of a kind. I have also had to embrace the fact that I too am different. Some people are so busy trying to keep up…that they are envious of someone who gets to be himself or herself. As I said before, this is part of God's plan. I trust in what he's trying to accomplish. I'm okay with the fact that I'm not like everyone else. I just want others to be okay with who I've become in the midst of this tragic whirlwind.

The world is stuck on what's familiar, what's popular, anything superficial, and what's not working; I believe we're due for a change. I for one am ready for it. Being stuck in the familiar, for me, would be like staying in my abusive ordeal, and I can't go back there. Your pain and your passion are connected to your purpose; find that line, and use it to climb out of the darkness. I'm in charge of how I feel, and today I choose happiness. You're not living if you can't be comfortable in your own skin. Don't be a slave to anything or anybody for the sake of image. You can't be who you used to be and who you're striving to become at the same time; you must make a choice and accept it. When you have fought so hard to get back on your feet, don't ever go back to the people who knocked you down. Never be defined by your past; it was just a lesson, not a life sentence. When you embrace your journey, no one can make you ashamed of it. No matter how much it hurts you now, someday you will look back and realize that your struggles changed your life for the better.

There's no force in this world that can hold down a determined person. The human soul cannot be permanently chained. Do what you feel in your heart to be true, and let the rest be unwritten; you're going to be criticized regardless. You can be misunderstood and still win!

God has put me through the hardest years of my life, showed me everyone's true colors, and made me stand alone. In other words, he's making me stronger, and for that I am forever grateful. I sit back and observe every person in my life, whether we talk every day or not. I know who motivates me, and I know who's bitterly honest with me. In addition, I know who talks about me and smiles in my face afterward. With that said, I no longer look for the good in people; I now search for the real instead. Because while good is often dressed in fake clothing, real is naked and proud, no matter the scars. What someone is willing to believe about you reveals the condition of that person's feelings toward you. False speculations and misperceptions of others lead to misled judgment, slander, and unwarranted gossip. I will always be a person who can be easily approached. Anything that anyone wants to know about Joseph Braxton, please feel free to ask; we all know where assumption leaves us. I've learned in this one lifetime that people don't take you seriously until someone else does. You'll eventually learn that you should stop waiting for their support and start working toward your goals despite the critics. Amazing things can happen when you distance yourself from the negativity. Some people are drawn to it; others learn lessons from it. What people don't understand is that no matter how educated, talented, rich, or cool you believe you are, how you treat people ultimately tells all; integrity is everything. You must be aware of people who are in your circle but not in your corner; know the difference.

I found myself crying out to many people, mainly the ones who claimed to be my friends. I expected them to be there for me, like I was there for them. Unfortunately, they were nowhere to be found, and that hurt. Now, don't get me wrong; there were a few who came to my rescue, and for that I am forever indebted. In life you'll find that no one notices your tears, no one notices your sadness, no one notices your pain, but they all notice your mistakes. Be willing to make them in plain sight. That way no one can tell you what you've done wrong; you'll already know.

From the start, I knew there was something different about me. I often enjoyed listening to music that had a deeper meaning than I understood. Songs like "Heal the World," "There's Got to Be a Way," "Earth Song," "Will You Be There," and "State of the World" gave me a natural high. I found myself listening carefully to the lyrics. A powerful song will have you in your feelings. I started imagining a world full of love and compassion, devoid of envy. Those types of thoughts always made me smile. Because I smiled, I was weird…because I was nice, I was weak. You'll learn that once a man becomes stronger in his faith, the flesh no longer influences his decisions. I'm imperfect; I know this. Some things I do may be a bit extreme, but the thought comes from a genuine place. To anyone whom I've rubbed the wrong way, let down, or disappointed, I sincerely apologize. Please don't hold any grudges; it's not healthy at all. And on a positive note, to anyone whom I've encouraged, empowered, or supported, thanks for keeping me going. You must know that you are important, whether or not you have the approval of others. Just because you've made some mistakes in the past does not mean you are one. Nobody's past is perfect. Some people will never forgive you, but never let that stop you from forgiving yourself.

I almost let go, but God kept me close to his heart. He placed his arms around me and used his hands to dry my tears. I am no longer afraid to live this life I've been given. There's many levels to living it, but I am constantly trying to overcome what has happened to me. Surrounding yourself with love is one of the most powerful remedies for getting through a traumatizing time in your life. You'll find yourself needing family and friends more than you ever have before. Loneliness becomes a sickness after a while and unbearable to live with. If you find that a loved one has been through sexual abuse or any other profound ordeal, try not to badger him or her. What such people need most of all is someone who will be there for them. My agonizing situation landed me in the psych ward: a place where I did not belong. Can you even imagine how it felt to be raped and then eventually punished for something that mentally changed your life? I have been roaming around the earth feeling like I'm constantly having an out-of-body experience. There is no way to shake sexual abuse off your person; it literally lives with you like the plague. I found myself encircled by negative people who tried to drain my positive way of living. They treated me like I was the carrier of a contagious disease. All I've ever wanted is to be treated like a human being. God did not make a mistake in his creation of me. I belong on this earth just as you feel you do. Anyone who has a true love for God will understand that loving humanity comes with the territory.

Loving and forgiving were two of the main issues I was having trouble with after my sexual assault. How can you love again after getting your heart ripped right out of your chest? Whom do you trust enough to develop a loving relationship with? A relationship of any kind was very hard for me to focus on after that. I often wondered if any of my childhood friends were being molested by the people they knew. There had to be at least one other person who had experienced such agony and pain; if there wasn't, then why had I? For years, all I'd been doing was observing my surroundings, too afraid to interact with anyone. There was no way life was supposed to be like this. I promised myself and God that if I ever made it through this turmoil in my life, I would dedicate the rest of my days to helping others overcome their battles if at all possible.

The loyalty that I offer during friendship is extremely strong. I'm not sure whether it's because of abandonment issues Robby placed on me or not. He constantly used me as his sex toy and then would leave me feeling shallow and alone till the next time.

Chapter One

Male Survivor

Writing this book has been a therapeutic yet painful experience for me. I've been holding in a lot of shame, and reliving what happened to me, in order to capture my life story, has stirred up all the things that I've been trying to forget. As a man, I was extremely afraid of what others would think of me. As a survivor, I'm blessed to still be alive and, well, to be able to tell my story. I went back and forth in my mind about how much of my life I should reveal in the book. I concluded that I needed to add as much as possible so that my readers could understand what I've truly been through. Besides, every sentence that I write and every word that I recite helps me live through the pain. Every day of my life has truly been a struggle for me. What you've seen as persons on the outside looking in is nothing compared to the front-row seat that I have been given. If I was asked to describe my ordeal in one word, I probably couldn't. There is no one word to describe sexual assault or molestation; and let's not forget that I've been through them both. In life we all have fears. Through my journey, I have discovered plenty of fears, ones that I never knew would surface. Losing my manhood, my masculinity, and my strength, and not being able to represent the true meaning of a man, just to name a few.

Society has many superficial opinions of what should take place in life and what shouldn't. That's why I try my best to stay positive when it comes to getting past my abuse. I constantly try to encourage guys who have been molested or abused to not be ashamed of what they've been through. I often find it funny that a person who's never walked a mile in your shoes would feel the need to make premature comments on how you should deal with life's shortcomings. I want every male out there to know that it's best to try to find a way to release the pain of what's hurt them without harming themselves or others and to never let what happened to them limit the fact that they are still as amazing a man as the day God created them. I learned early on after my abuse that people will pass judgment until something detrimental happens to them. Then they want your compassion and your honest opinion on how they should handle their situation, or they may not want you to comment at all. Regardless, they've forgotten how harsh they were when you were going through your own tragedy.

There are many people in the world with selfish hearts. They live in glass houses that of course they would never want you to throw stones at. Always remember that God is key in every aspect of your life. Just learning more every day about how people are lets me further know that I made the right decision about getting closer to the Lord. There is no one person in the world who is above help, or shall I say beyond help. I use to feel that because I waited so long to tell someone what happened to me, no one would believe me, let alone help me. If you read my story and discover that you either have been through a similar ordeal or know someone who has, all I ask is that you never give up. If you can muster up any type of strength to ask for help, please do so. If no one else knows, I know that it's easier said than done, but please try. I lost a lot of years being afraid; I wouldn't want you to suffer like I did. The control that my victimizer had over me was more than suffocating; I was desperate for help. I felt like I couldn't swim and kept lifting my head above water to reach out for someone to save me. And every time I did, I felt like no one was there. I later found out that I was uttering the words "Help me," and no one could hear them, because I wasn't saying it loud enough. It was as if I was practicing the whole time. I realized that my lack of faith in God was crushing my voice box. I tell you one thing: once my faith got stronger, God restored my windpipe.

There are so many of you out there suffering from this type of abuse, or even worse. Just the thought of knowing that saddens my heart. Just letting go of the loneliness of it all is a pleasant feeling. Not knowing who to tell led to many days alone. I didn't know how to be around other people without feeling sad or diminished. I thought isolating myself would help my situation, but it didn't; it actually made it worse. I slowly but surely found myself spiraling out of control, to the point of no return. It was as if I were hang gliding without a parachute to release. I ventured into things that I knew nothing about just to release the pain. At one point I felt like the devil and I were best friends—metaphorically, but it felt true to life for me. When I say that I was lost, I *was* lost.

Every other line that I write, I recite to myself, "I survived," and then I continue to type. I'm sharing all the details of my journey through all of this. I'm giving you the rundown of what's on my mind while I'm writing. It feels so damn good to be here on this heavenly earth to describe the ins and outs of my abuse, my conquest to overcome abuse, domestic violence, and misfortune. How wonderful it truly feels that, during my healing process, I am able to assist someone else. Oh joyful, joyful Lord, I thank you for my Godly heart and the flesh that you give me to spread your blessings throughout the universe. Oh Lord, I promised you that if you would save me from such turmoil and pain, I would live out the rest of my days in your faith and glory. Oh Father God, where would I be if I didn't have you by my side? I am the man who I am today because of you, Father God. Let the wisdom that you've given me be my eternal guide. May I go into your will with a clear mind and an understanding heart. Amen.

> Trust in the Lord with all your heart; do not depend on your own understanding. Seek his will in all you do, and he will show you which path to take.
>
> (Prov. 3:5–6)

> Then Jesus said, "Come to me, all of you who are weary and carry heavy burdens, and I will give you rest."
>
> (Matt. 11:28)

If you or someone you know has experienced sexual assault or domestic violence, you can call to speak to a counselor or be referred to local services: National Sexual Assault Hotline, 1-800-656-4673. For male survivors of childhood sexual abuse, visit 1in6's online support line: 1in6.org/men/get-help. For the National Domestic Violence Hotline, call 1-800-799-7233. To find local resources and information about domestic violence, search the online database at domesticshelters.org. For the Teen Dating Violence Hotline, call 1-866-331-9474 or text "loveis" to 22522. Their website is www.loveisrespect.org.

Chapter Two

Courage to Heal

It has taken a lot of strength, faith, and courage to make it to this day. Believe me, it has truly been tough wondering how the world would accept what I needed to let go. There are several questions that I've asked myself through the years, and now I'm going to ask my readers the same ones: Will you feel the need to judge me for being a man who has been violated by another man for so long? Will you judge me for then feeling guilty for pretty much giving into his volatile ways, or will you factor fear into your opinion of me? Will you look down on me, or will you put yourself in my shoes, because you are truly aware that molestation and sexual assault do not have a particular person in mind that they choose to destroy? Will you find my story an inspiration for you or for someone you know, or will you shun the fact that my story even exists, solely because you or someone you know has been through the same thing? Courage has been my divine intervention for as long as I can remember. I just didn't know whom

I could trust to tell my story to; so I told no one. I was confused; I was stressed, but I knew I was ready to be free from all the madness. I had to find the power and the strength within to release what's been holding me back for so many years. I found myself missing out on so much because of my abuse. I went out of my way to do as much as I could to prepare myself for healing. I had to cut the abuser off without a shadow of a doubt, and then I had to push myself to be a fighter. So when I tell you that I'm ready, I am more than ready to finally live a life that I truly deserve.

When you've been wronged by someone you thought you could trust, you begin to harbor a lot of distasteful feelings, such as resentment. If you're not careful, resentment can force you to hold grudges. Grudges are sins that are put in line by the devil to steal your ability to trust anyone. One thing to always remember: even if it's just one person in your life, you need to be able to trust. I know that the human flesh is unreliable; however, God uses humans to distribute his blessings. I had a close friend in my corner when I was going through my abuse. Sometimes when I think back, I realize that if I didn't have that person or the unconditional love from my mother, I wouldn't be the survivor that I'm presenting to you today. Living life is sometimes awkward enough without having someone to vent to from time to time. If nothing else, you might need to indulge in a listening ear to get you through. Take it from me; after going through a terrible, volatile situation, you will tend to feel like you are losing your mind. You'll always need to reach out to someone on the outside looking in to help you feel sane again. I definitely needed someone to help prove that this abuse didn't take my sanity from me. That also brings me to the fact that holding on to something that belongs solely to you is also appropriately needed for the survival mission.

After the actual abuse takes place, it's like you go through an unforgettable meltdown. You get this overwhelming sense of feeling like a mere weakling. You find yourself fighting with the notion of why you weren't able to prevent the attack, and then why you weren't able to protect yourself from the attack. Needless to say, I'm not able to speak for everyone's bout with sexual abuse, but I guarantee you that someone out there will resonate with what I've shared about my life, and why I've been so guarded for so long.

Molestation and rape brought on addictions. Addictions that I'm not too happy about, but addictions nevertheless. I developed a fascination for sex. It was the act of it, the sight of it, the climax of sex, and the action of it. I would stay home alone so that it wouldn't take over me. I grew an addiction to porn, and often I would masturbate to the thought of sex. I'm not proud of this addiction; however, I'm trying to be as honest as I possibly can about the changes that sexual abuse can cause. I work hard daily to get over my addictions. Once you start to get rid of one addiction, you arbitrarily adapt to another one. When I finally got in touch with why I developed the addiction to sex and porn, I started on my road to getting over it. My fascination with porn came from seeing someone other than myself being dominated. As I said before, all these feelings and thoughts come from my actual abuse. Now that I have learned how to tame the thrill of sex, my new affliction is shopping for shoes. I've even narrowed it down to two brands: Cole Haan and Puma Suede. My new addictions don't stop there; I also am addicted to materials and fabrics that are used for Lapels4acause. Everything that I can find positive in my life, I use as a self-help to healing. Healing from sexual abuse doesn't stop just because time has moved on; it becomes a lifelong process.

I can actually say with a straight face that I hate what has happened to me. But in the next breath, I can tell you all that the person I am today has more than risen to the occasion of what God has prepared me for in spite of it all. I won't lie and say I'm completely healed from it. The one thing that I can say is that this journey has been one like no other. I've learned lessons that only God could have taught me. Now there has been this feeling in me for years that I'm not sure will ever leave my soul. It's the fear of it happening again. Of course, it's not something I try to think about on a daily basis, but it's part of the new thought process that I have been given from the assault. No matter how I try to shake off what happened to me, I can't. The life I live every day and the things that are not only brought to my attention but are happening around me show me that there are still people in the world cruel enough to hurt me in that manner again. Maybe not the same person, but a person who has been dealt a dirty hand in life and feels the need to take out his or her misery on a person like me. I'm no one's punching bag, and I refuse to let the abuse turn me back into a person who I never wanted to become in the first place. I'm a man who understands that everyone has issues in their lives. I understand because I too have some of those same issues; judgment from me, you will never receive. I'm just so blessed to still be around to write this story about my life.—a life that I never knew would be full of so many awesome things to see and so many lessons to learn.

The world we live in is not what's corrupt; it's the people who live in the world who are corrupt. I think that everyone deserves a chance to be redeemed of their sins. I don't want to live a life full of hatred. I want to make the rest of my life, the best of my life. God gave me more than a second chance to do his will correctly. I have no choice but to recognize that and embrace the concept of his plan. God only knows that the thought of my abuse still hurts at times, but like the serenity prayer, "God grant me the serenity to accept the things I cannot change, courage to change the things I can, and wisdom to know the difference." With that said, there is no need for me to continue spending more time on something

I can't do anything about. A relationship with God will change so much more in your life than you could even imagine. The will to want to build a relationship with him will lead you on a path unknown to humankind. My relationship with God is personal, but it is definitely worth praising. I shock myself sometimes when I think about how far I've come. It has been a great blessing and truly an unavoidable lesson. Molestation and sexual abuse are calamities that you can't just bounce back from. That's why tenacity is very important to gain in order to get through your tragedy.

Courage to me means more than what *Webster's Dictionary* could define it as. Everyone's venture to find courage will be different. It is something that you will only be able to describe from within. It took me many years to find the strength to even develop courage. I truly believe that there are levels to becoming free from any type of abuse. Developing courage is a difficult and complex process by itself, let alone trying to find a healing mechanism. Healing is housed deep inside you; it forms shelter in your heart. It is first based on forgiving the damage that was done, so that you can even attempt to heal.

The hardest part about trying to heal was having to face things. Face what was bothering me, face what was hindering me from living my life, face what took my voice away, face myself, and face changes that had to be made in order to live happily. What I've learned firsthand is that you have to pray for the forgiveness of your victimizer; in return God will forgive you for your wrongdoings. Without being able to forgive the person who hurt you, you'll never truly be able to move on from the infliction. You will block God's up-and-coming blessings for you. I gained courage when the depression pushed me to rock bottom. Rock bottom meaning I had lost everything. I was at my last stretch and did not want to keep breathing. Talking to someone with a listening ear, prayer, faith, support, and wanting to finally live a life while there was breath still in me were other ways I was able to muster up any form of courage.

Who I am and what I stand for go much further than my abuse. I want my book to be an inspiration to you all. My goal is to reach millions with my story. I'm sure there are several people in several cities as well as countries who have been through a similar situation. I am truly blessed to be here to help as many people as I possibly can. The road to courage and healing has not been an easy one for me, as I've mentioned before, but I am fighting every day to get through it. Another thing that I want others to be sure of is that prayer truly works. God has heard my cry and has listened to my pleading when I thought no one else would. To acknowledge him is to truly love him.

For if you forgive other people when they sin against you, your heavenly father will also forgive you. But if you do not forgive others their sins, your father will not forgive your sins.

(Matt. 6:14–15)

Be strong and courageous. Do not be afraid or terrified because of them, for the lord your god goes with you; he will never leave you nor forsake you.

(Deut. 31:6)

Chapter Three

Prisoner

Mentally, physically, emotionally, literally, and figuratively, I've been a prisoner…

Mentally, I was conditioned by the pain of depression to never want to live fully. I let depression invade my space and force me into not wanting to experience any type of happiness. Everything that could possibly come to mind did when I was behind bars. Thoughts of not getting out crossed my mind several times, but I knew I had to do something to change my frame of mind. The mind is one of the strongest parts of the body; in all actuality it controls it. If you give in to what's causing pain around you, you'll never be able to survive a detrimental ordeal. I knew that mentally I would never be the same again. It's not just who you were before you got in trouble with the law; it's who you're afraid to become during your stay in the correctional facility. I was afraid of who I would become. Mentally you need something to hold on to. I held onto the fact that my life was worth more than this bout with justice. If I could just get out, I could work on changing my way of living; those words were constantly playing over and over in my head.

Physically I locked myself away from everyone; I wasn't too trusting. I would never let anyone get close to me, no matter who they were. I now know that this was a continuation of the mental state I was in. No matter what anyone tells you, there is no possible way to wash the prison feel off your skin; it's embedded. It leaves a scar that can't even be surgically removed. The only advice that I can give is, never wear it as a coat of armor. The moment you are released, make the proper arrangements to go and get some type of counseling. There are certain things in life that you should never try to heal from on your own. Please know that counseling is not as bad as everyone makes it out to be. If you're really interested in becoming a better person after it's all said and done, you must further understand that change takes time, dedication, hope, faith, and patience.

Emotionally my mind was all over the place. I felt like I had to watch everything and everyone around me in order to survive. I used my kindness to gain the respect of a group of prisoners who could possibly protect me. I knew how long I was going to be in there; therefore, I knew I had to think wisely. One thing I know for sure is that you never want to make enemies in a place surrounded by people who live their lives on the edge. Prison is not a place where you will ever feel or be comfortable. It's not your home, and you must always remember that. That phrase alone will keep you focused on what's important while you're there. It is all about survival of the fittest. In some instances, it's kill or be killed. I knew that I didn't belong there, so I did not want to give in to the prison mentality. I had family who loved me, and the plan was to get out and go be with them. There was nothing that interested me enough to want to stay behind bars and lose focus on what was important. If nothing else, I knew I couldn't keep putting my mother through this.

Literally, I was trying to fill certain voids with temporary highs. I found myself involved in mentally and physically abusive relationships where I did whatever they asked me to do because I felt like I had no choice. I eventually started following the wrong crowds to fill more painful voids, which landed me in prison. The funny thing was that I felt safer in prison because I was away from my abuser and didn't have to face the world with my shame. On the other hand, I was extremely miserable without my freedom. Prison is not a place for anyone who is trying to change for the better; it was hell for me. Just imagine all day every day not having anything to do but read and stare at three walls and a locked door. Maybe place a call to your family if possible. During the week we had a certain day to place our commissary order and then there was a day designated to issuing our items to us. On that day, we weren't able to place calls or come out of our cells. Sometimes those were the longest twenty-four hours of my life. I would rather place a call to my mother than receive commissary.

In other aspects of prison life, you're made to feel like a slave; at least it felt like that to me. If nothing else, karma makes you think. Being institutionalized will make you realize all you've taken for granted. Can you imagine long periods of time not being with the ones you love and missing holidays, birthdays, and funerals? Oh my, and the food was despicable. The names of the food alone would make you not want to eat it. "Shit on the shingle" and "cow tongue"—where in the world did those names come from, and why on God's green earth would anyone think of feeding another human being that crap? I understand that I was a prisoner awarded to the state; however, I was still a human being, and I'm sure at times the correctional officers as well as the prison guards noticed. Taking showers became a luxury while in prison. In order to take one, you had to stand in line and wait for everyone else to finish. Of course, that was only if you wanted to take one alone. The water was extremely hot, and I had to constantly watch my surroundings to avoid being raped. Another thing I tried to avoid was getting in a relationship with another inmate. I hated seeing men in prison.

Prison was a gay man's paradise, but it was embarrassing for me. They sought out vulnerable prisoners whom they could pretend with during their stay, and then they'd get out of jail and continue to live heterosexual lives. They'd pretend that they never met you just because it was back to the basics. I don't have anything against brothers on the down low; I just want them to understand that being on the down low or discreetly bisexual can sometimes make people seem extremely dishonest, and they have to watch that. It's like they live a double life, and it changes them into someone else. I want them all to understand that they are not alone when having feelings for the same sex; they just have to be careful, because other people can get hurt in the long run.

Rest didn't come easy in the prison system. I had to constantly watch my back, especially because of being surrounded by lifers. Every day I constantly thought about the fact that I wasn't raised to live my life in this manner. Being on the inside gave me all the time in the world to think about my mistakes. You try to keep hope alive about what your future could be like if you could just redeem yourself and get out. I won't deny that after a while depression sets in; trying to avoid it is the most trying thing ever. And of course, once you show signs of unhappiness, that's when they want to pump you full of pills.

When I was out committing crimes, I wasn't thinking about the impact it had on my loved ones. I'm still harboring guilt to this day for taking my mother through so much. No one ever talks about what happens to the families on the outside—how they may feel about their loved ones being away from civilization for so long. Not being able to communicate with them for days at a time, having to express everything to them in one call before the operator comes on the phone and says you have just a little time left, not knowing when you'll be able to hear their voices again—it's extremely hard to act unbothered by something so painful. I remember calling my mother crying about the things that I watched happen in and out of my cell. I wanted it all to be over as soon as possible.

I wouldn't wish imprisonment on anyone. Some days I wonder how I even made it through one day, let alone a whole year. I kept to myself most of the time, not really wanting to have eye-to-eye contact. I'd heard many stories about how easy it was to provoke someone on the inside. I still remember my first week on the tier; I witnessed a guy getting hit with a lock in a sock. The blood from his injury was profusely flowing out the back of his head. It was at that moment I realized that jail was not a place for me. How do you manage to stay in a place where you know you don't belong and not get caught up in mayhem? I had no prior experience with being locked down to this degree. And even though there are other inmates, jail is still one of the loneliest places. Prison wasn't the answer for me; I needed help from a therapist. Jail is never the answer. Many are imprisoned for reasons that are unexplainable. Some crimes that individuals commit are just cries for help. I can't speak for all of them, but I've lost friendships through my actions. I would never let anyone get close to me for fear of being prejudged. I've judged myself enough all these years. I've never felt good enough for anything or anyone.

Figuratively, I have been sailing through this long journey of depression, just dealing with life's ups and downs. I had to face the fact that I was a prisoner in life long before I became a prisoner of the state. I finally broke through the chains that had been weighing me down for so long. If you allow your past to haunt you, you will be forever a prisoner. Slowly but surely I started regaining my self-worth. It was extremely hard to have my freedom taken away from me only to be identified as a prison ID number. Even though I felt safe from what was going on in my life, I was miserable. Losing your freedom is a prison by itself; it's precious time that you can't get back. Just remember that everyone makes mistakes; some get caught, and some don't. Let your wake-up call be your testimony. Make a vow to yourself to be the inspiration that the world needs to see in order to know that change can happen if you want it badly enough. Peace is the presence of now without judgment.

> The light shines in the darkness, and the darkness can never extinguish it.
>
> (John 1:5 [NLT])
>
> Judgments are prepared for scoffers and beatings for the backs of fools.
>
> (Prov. 19:29 [NKJV])

Chapter Four

Afraid of Kindness

I have spent many years masking my pain by being overly kind to others. I felt I didn't deserve to be treated nicely in return. I believed I was obligated to treat everyone in the best way humanly possible. I gave so much of myself that I didn't have anything left to give. On the outside looking in, it may seem like I have it all together or am materialistic; however, actually, it's a complete cover-up. I let what I did for others drain and deprive me of the kindness I deserved. I am my own worst enemy, and I'm tired of accepting that.

Trust is one of the main reasons why I shied away from other people's gentleness. After what I'd been through, I couldn't help but doubt people's compassion. Why would I expect people to be sincere about their kind gestures toward me, when I had allowed myself to be mistreated on a daily basis? I didn't feel like I had any sense of direction

Joe Braxton

at the time. I am an adult now, and I still find life to be a mystery. There seems to be a hidden agenda in the minds of uncontrolled spectators. I've seen the expression on people's faces when they weren't sure of how to take me. They've prejudged me in their own way, and in some ways I've allowed them to.

What I've grown accustomed to as far as the behavior of others is all that I have to go by. Until I was shown differently, I didn't know any different. We all are the directors of our own screenplays; you only can be taken seriously by the script that you've written for your life. I knew that I couldn't allow myself to keep being treated differently. I told myself constantly that I needed to write a new script to tell the true story of who I am. After a while I truly enjoyed being around others, and my trust issues went away slowly but surely. However, I always try to watch my surroundings, and I watch the company that I keep at all times. I have to make sure that I can decipher who's for me and who's against me. Knowledge for some is just a state of mind; to others it's what's obtained in textbooks, and to me it's being able to know the difference between what or who is real and what or who is fake.

Moving forward, my journey will be about giving more of myself to others. I've chosen to rest assured that God will watch over the naysayers for me. I can't worry about those who don't want to join my positive movement. It has taken me long enough to sift through the bad and the good of others. I can't keep allowing myself to return to a place that I never wanted to be in. I pray that with my continuous acts of kindness, who I really am will shine through. The struggle to return to your natural state of mind is real. Who I was before my sexual abuse is not who I am now. Then I was a defenseless child; today I am a man who has survived adversity. I can't actually say if my fight to regain who I was will ever be over. However, what I can say is that I will never stop trying to find the part of me that went missing in the midst of it all. I'm no longer torturing myself or others around me because of what I've been through. I know now that it is no more their fault than it is mine.

We will never know nor will we understand what God has planned for our lives unless we ask. Instead of constantly asking him, "Why me?" change that question to "What's my next move?" Your faith in him will stop you from questioning his work. What's meant for you will come to you. There is not one human being alive who can take away the direction that God has led you in. The temptation to do what you see others do will always be there. Your true test of faith is asking God to remove those who try to persuade you to go down the wrong path with them. When your flesh begins to feel weak, read the good book. When you feel that's not enough, get on your hands and knees. Humble yourself in front of the Lord, and your prayers will be received. He did not guide you this far to leave you stagnated. Understand that your faith in him and someone else's faith in him will never be the same. Don't ever take that time to prejudge anyone; love them regardless. It never matters if people understand why you're being kind to them in spite of what they may have done to you. It only matters that God can see your growth from the gifts that he has given you.

Am I scared of what people may say or think of me after reading my story? That thought crosses my mind from time to time, but shortly thereafter it fades away. No more dwelling on the opinions of others. It's time to face the music and learn how to cope with the new rhythm of my life. I have been afraid for far too long, and the buck stops here. I'm learning how to be okay with the opinions of others. The goal is to make better choices for my life. I'm no longer interested in wallowing in my sorrows. What I tell myself daily is that I need to be all right within myself in order to be comfortable helping others get through their trying times. I know how badly I wanted someone to assist me with my sexually abusive situation; I also know how painful it was to not be able to ask anyone for help. I remember every painful moment, and I know how hard it's been for me to live past it. I can't expect others to do the same; I can only try to assist with the process.

It hurts, dammit; it truly does, and you will never hear me say that it doesn't. I would be lying if I even uttered those words. I'm sure that when I listen to others tell their story, I may even weep for them. And that's okay; it's a human emotion when you hear something that plays on a trigger in your life. Only the strongest can survive, and I am extremely strong. On the days that I thought I wasn't, God showed me how wrong I was.

I'll let you in on a little secret. Recently my victimizer contacted me in reference to my story. We talked, but it was over the phone. I know that it should have been in person; nevertheless, we talked. I wasn't expecting to hear from him, but I feel as though I handled it well. I told him, in every way imaginable, how what he did to me destroyed my life. He has actually convinced himself that it wasn't that bad. For those reasons alone, I have created the toughest shield that I now wear around me. It's a shield that I want to have pierced, but I'm afraid that I wouldn't know how to deal with it.

I was more than afraid of kindness, because I didn't feel worthy of it. However, I have given so much of who I am to others that I now understand why kindness is truly needed. I constantly watch the faces of people whom I've helped or given a tidbit of wisdom to. They are eternally grateful for the smallest thing that I contributed to their lives. It puts one of the biggest smiles on my face. It gives me a reason to keep doing it: it's a part of the hope that I offer myself to keep going. Who are we really if we don't feel compelled to hold onto reasons to live? I wanted to give up a long time ago.

There was a time in my life when it didn't matter what someone said to me in a positive manner; I wanted to end it all. I didn't see or feel any of the things that people were saying to me. I saw a different shade of myself in the mirror. There was always a gray area in my life. I never felt like the grass was greener on the other side, and no one could convince me that it was. I felt so dead inside. After a while I started feeling that I wasn't a good person—boy, was I wrong! I've been walking around with a demon of sorts on my shoulder. It's a constant battle every day to get rid of it. Wearing it allows my past to stop me from wanting something different, but I'm never going to give up. Once I found out that God continues to love you even after you've sinned, it was like a weight had been lifted off my shoulders.

I love myself in spite of who people think I am. I need to love myself in spite of who people think I am. I have learned that it doesn't matter who shows up in your life; you must find the strength to always be there for yourself. As long as God wakes me up every day, I am accounted for. *I am living for myself.* It feels really good to type these words.. I am a living testimony that change is good, and forgiveness is better. Every paragraph that I write and every sentence that I reread is real to me. I am here; I am a child of God, and therefore I am truly loved; there is no other way to put it. When you're coming from a place of forever sadness, constant brutality, and everlasting pain, you learn to appreciate the true meaning of life. As I've said before and I will never hesitate to say again, my name is Joseph Braxton, and I am a survivor of molestation and sexual abuse, but I am *still breathing.*

Look at God…

But let all that take refuge in you be glad, let them ever sing for joy; and may you shelter them, that those who love your name may exult in you.

(Ps. 5:11)

How blessed is the one whom you choose and bring near to you to dwell in your courts? We will be satisfied with the goodness of your house, your holy temple.

(Ps. 65:4)

Made in the USA
San Bernardino, CA
24 July 2017